Leaving the Earth

I0811894

By Eamonn Corrigan

Code Breakers

Suffixes (-able, -ee, -er, -ist, -less, -or, -y)

Scan this code to access the Teacher's Notes for this series or visit
www.norwoodhousepress.com/decodables

Norwood House Press

DEAR CAREGIVER, *Code Breakers* is a series designed to support readers who have mastered basic decoding skills and are moving into the later alphabetic and consolidated phase of reading. Through carefully selected words and high-interest topics, each book allows upper elementary readers the opportunity to practice advanced phonics patterns and morphemes with engaging, age-appropriate text.

Each book has an accompanying teacher's guide. This guide provides an explicit lesson plan following a systematic routine for teaching phonemic awareness, phonics, decoding, and fluency. It provides opportunities to increase vocabulary and build syntactic skills that support comprehension. The lessons are aligned with standards addressing foundational language and literacy skills.

When reading these books with your child, encourage them to sound out words that are unfamiliar by breaking larger words into syllables and then attending to the target letter(s) and sounds. If the unknown word is an irregularly spelled high-frequency word, you may encourage your child to attend to the known parts of the word and provide the pronunciation of the unknown part(s). Rereading the texts multiple times will allow your child the opportunity to build their reading fluency, a skill necessary for proficient comprehension.

You can be confident you are providing your child with opportunities to build their decoding abilities, which will encourage their independence as they become lifelong readers.

Happy Reading!

Emily Nudds, M.S.Ed Literacy
Literacy Consultant

Norwood House Press • www.norwoodhousepress.com

Printed in the United States of America.
378N–082024

Library of Congress Cataloging-in-Publication Data has been filed and is available at https://lccn.loc.gov/2024010763
Literacy Consultant: Emily Nudds, M.S.Ed Literacy
Editorial and Production Development and Management: Focus Strategic Communications Inc.
Editors: Christine Gaba, Christi Davis-Martell

Photo Credits: NASA (pp. 7, 9, 11, 13); Shutterstock: Macrovector (covers), Paopano (p. 17); Wikimedia Commons (pp. 5, 15, 19, 21).

Hardcover ISBN: 978-1-6845-0175-5 Paperback ISBN: 978-1-6845-0174-8
eBook ISBN: 978-1-6845-0176-2

Contents

Chapter 1
The Dream of the Stars

Before the age of rocketry, astronomers looked to the sky. With their telescopes and boundless curiosity, these early visionaries were pioneers who had a dream of a journey among the stars.

Among these dreamers was Galileo. He was an astronomer who, with his simple telescope, unveiled the Moon's **craggy** landscape. The cosmos no longer felt so far away. Was it more attainable? Following in his footsteps was the theorist Konstantin Tsiolkovsky, sometimes called the "Father of **Astronautics**." Tsiolkovsky was a scientist whose theories predicted much of modern rocket science.

This book celebrates the limitless achievements of stargazers and devotees of the cosmos. These were the people whose dreamy visions inspired countless others to look up and wonder, too.

Did You Know?

The idea of a "space elevator," a tower reaching from Earth to space, was first imagined by Tsiolkovsky in 1895. This visionary concept has inspired scientists and engineers to explore new ways of reaching the stars.

Konstantin Tsiolkovsky, a Russian rocket scientist, is considered one of the founders of astronautics.

Chapter 2
Rocket Pioneers

Our journey to space made valuable progress due to the work of Dr. Robert H. Goddard. Goddard was an American engineer who created the world's first liquid-fueled rocket. Launched in 1926, the rocket flew just a short distance. Yet it must have left the observers speechless. To witness such an achievement would surely have been an enjoyable experience.

Then came Wernher von Braun, a German rocket builder who dreamed of the stars. He was a co-developer of the V-2 rocket. This became the first **artificial** object to travel into space in 1944.

These pioneers showed us that flying beyond the clouds was not a hopeless effort.

Did You Know?

Goddard's first rocket in 1926 might have been small, but it was an unbeliev<u>able</u> start. It flew a reason<u>able</u> 184 feet (56 meters). That's almost as long as half a football field!

Dr. Robert H. Goddard is seen beside his early rocket in 1926, showing the humble beginnings of space travel.

Chapter 3
The First Astronauts

The leap into space began with brave explorers Americans call astronauts. Yuri Gagarin, a daring adventurer from the **Soviet Union**, became the very first space voyager. He orbited Earth in 1961. His journey was a measurable leap for all of us.

One month later, American Alan Shepard soared into space, becoming an innovator in his own right. Shepard steered his craft, making him the conductor of the first human-piloted space flight.

These missions helped scientists to understand space better. Every astronaut is an educator and investigator. We now better understand the universe around us due to the countless **contributions** of these astronauts.

Did You Know?

Gagarin's trip to space took only 108 minutes from ignition to landing. Imagine circling the whole planet in less time than it takes to watch a movie!

Yuri Gagarin, the first human in space, is shown on his way to the launch pad on April 12, 1961.

Chapter 4
The Space Race

The 1960s were a time of rapid technological advancements in space travel. When Yuri Gagarin and Alan Shepard went into space, the United States and the Soviet Union were locked in a restless race to improve their space programs. This was dubbed the "Space Race."

Both countries built better, faster rockets. They sent more explorers into space. They were competitors, but this contest made them strive to achieve more. The **pessimists** around the world saw this as a waste of money which could lead to avoidable accidents. The excitable **optimists** saw this as the future of humanity.

Astronauts became the fashionable heroes of this era. During this decade, these adventurers orbited Earth, walked in space, and tested new technology to improve rocketry. This was all due to their bravery and the sleepless nights of hardworking scientists and engineers.

Did You Know?

During the Space Race, humans saw Earth from space for the first time. The astronauts looked at Earth from space and took pictures that were shared with the world. These pictures showed Earth as a beautiful, fragile orb, and forever changed how we see our planet.

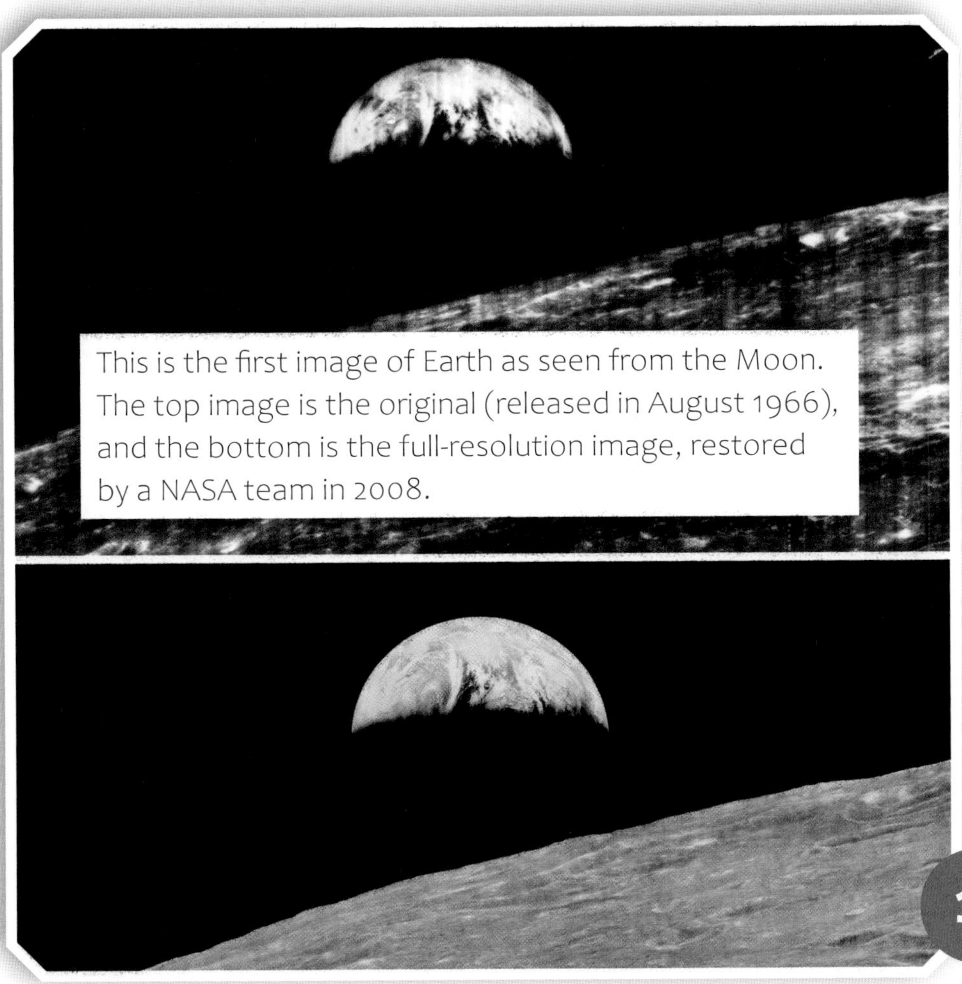

This is the first image of Earth as seen from the Moon. The top image is the original (released in August 1966), and the bottom is the full-resolution image, restored by a NASA team in 2008.

Chapter 5
Moon Walkers

The greatest dream imaginable during the Space Race was to walk on the Moon. In 1969, that dream finally became reality. The Apollo 11 mission made history when astronauts Neil Armstrong and Buzz Aldrin became the first humans to set foot on the Moon. As Armstrong stepped onto the Moon's dusty surface, he said the now recognizable line: "That's one small step for man, one giant leap for mankind."

This timeless moment was watched by millions of people around the world. The astronauts were investigators, photographers, and collectors of Moon rocks. Their work continues to help **physicists** and **geologists** learn more about the Moon.

The Apollo missions continued until 1972. During this time, 10 more people walked on the Moon. Each mission was a reliable source of new discoveries. These Moon walkers were brave explorers, leading the way into space.

Did You Know?

There is no atmosphere on the Moon, so there is no wind or rain to erase footprints. The marks left by the Apollo astronauts could last for millions of years!

The historic first steps on the Moon were made by Apollo 11 astronauts.

Chapter 6
The Space Shuttle Era

Exploration in space entered a new phase with the Space Shuttle. Space Shuttles were largely reusable. This made them much cheaper to run than other programs, which also meant more regular trips to space. We started sending more specialists to space for experiments, too. These specialists included **botanists**, physicists, and analysts.

The first Shuttle, named *Columbia*, flew in 1981. This proved that repeated space travel (unlike a rocket) was manageable. For the next 30 years, we used the Shuttle to fix changeable satellites, conduct tricky science experiments, and slowly build the previously unimaginable International Space Station (ISS).

Many people flew on the Shuttle. Their relentless efforts made enormous contributions to space exploration.

Did You Know?

In 1990, the Space Shuttle *Discovery* was used to launch the Hubble Space Telescope into Earth's orbit. Hubble lets us see faraway galaxies and study icy worlds in our solar system. It is one of the greatest scientific achievements of all time.

This is an image of the Space Shuttle *Discovery* taking off on October 23, 2007, for STS-120. This was the 120th mission of the Space Shuttle Era.

Chapter 7
Life in Orbit

One of the most unbelievable accomplishments in human space exploration is the International Space Station (ISS). The ISS means we can live in space for extended periods of time. In fact, some astronauts have stayed for more than a year at a time. The ISS is like a giant science lab, available for us to conduct experiments outside Earth.

Astronauts live a very minimalist life on the ISS. It is difficult to bring supplies, so only the essentials needed to make astronauts comfortable are sent. Astronauts feel weightless while the ISS orbits Earth. This means they float around the ISS, not walk.

Life up there is busy, too. Astronauts are constantly working on experiments or repairing and improving the ISS systems. Some experiments have tested which plants are growable in space. Others seek to better understand how we can make life in space more **sustainable**.

Did You Know?

Astronauts on the ISS see 16 sunrises (and sunsets) every day because the station orbits Earth every 90 minutes!

This view of Earth is seen from a window on the International Space Station.

Chapter 8
New Space Pioneers

In recent years, most trips to space are not made by government-owned space agencies like NASA. Now, hireable companies such as SpaceX or Blue Origin are widely used. If you pay them, they will be the operator of your very own flight to space.

Astronauts traveling to the ISS from NASA or other space agencies often travel on SpaceX rockets. They are more affordable than launching their own rockets. This was a big leap, showing that private rockets were relatively harmless and could carry people into space safely, reliably, and economically.

Right now, space tourism is a luxury. A short trip costs between $500,000 and $1.5 million. However, there are many people who are willing to pay this to be space travelers. Space travel companies hope to promote space tourism and make it more affordable. Perhaps one day, you may not need to be a millionaire, or a NASA trainee or employee, to become an astronaut yourself.

Did You Know?

Astronauts sleeping in space have to attach themselves to something, so they don't float around the ship and bang into equipment! They sleep in cozy, floating sleeping bags often attached to the wall.

A SpaceX rocket booster attempts to land in 2015.

Chapter 9
The Next Frontier

Over the past 100 years, we have transitioned from cheery observers to visitors of space. From Goddard's early rocketry to Yuri Gagarin's historic windy flight to regular trips to space, we have reached new heights. Today's space pioneers are making the galaxy more accessible to all devotees.

In the coming decades, humans hope to return to the rocky Moon, a destination we have not visited for 50 years. Mars, a small red dot in the sky, is becoming an achievable goal. Traveling to space, which was once thought unreachable, is now marked with our footprints.

Each starry-eyed astronaut and every optimistic engineer builds upon the progress of our predecessors. Space invites the next generation of explorers to travel to the stars in new and exciting ways.

This image of Buzz Aldrin on the Moon was taken by Neil Armstrong during the Apollo 11 mission in 1969.

Glossary

artificial: not naturally occurring; made by human beings

astronautics (ăs-trə-nŏ-tĭks): the science of human space travel

botanists (bŏ-tən-ĭsts): scientists who study plants

contributions: parts played by humans for a larger project

craggy: describing a rough and uneven surface, such as a cliff face

geologists: scientists who study Earth and rocks

optimists: those who tend to view the best aspects of things or expect good things to happen

pessimists: those who tend to view the worst aspects of things or expect bad things to happen

physicists: scientists who study matter and energy to better understand how the universe functions

Soviet Union: a large country spanning much of Europe and some of Asia from 1922–1991. Much of the Soviet Union is now the country of Russia.

sustainable (sə-stā-nə-bəl): can be kept up or continued for a long time